The WHITE MOUNTAINS

A PHOTOGRAPHIC PORTRAIT

First published in the United States of America by
PilotPress Publishers, Inc., James R. Franklin, Publisher
110 Westchester Road
Newton, Massachusetts 02458
Telephone: (617) 332-0703
www.PilotPress.com
and
Twin Light Publishers, Inc., Doris R. Patey, Publisher
Ten Hale Street
Rockport, Massachusetts 01966
Telephone: (978) 546-7398
http://www.twinlightspub.com

ISBN 1-885435-10-X

10 9 8 7 6 5 4 3 2 1

Designer: Leeann Leftwich
          Email: clldesign@aol.com

Cover image: Michael Hubley

Printed in China

The WHITE MOUNTAINS

A PHOTOGRAPHIC PORTRAIT

PILOTPRESS PUBLISHERS · TWIN LIGHTS PUBLISHERS

SWIFT RIVER
1869
TOWN OF CONWAY, NEW

TABLE *of* CONTENTS

Foreword   6

Southern White Mountains   12

Western White Mountains   42

Northern White Mountains   70

Eastern White Mountains   84

Acknowledgments   127

Index of Photographers   128

Robert Hamilton

The Swift River Bridge in Conway no longer carries vehicles, just powerful memories of a time when clever men and big wooden posts and beams were all you needed to cross a river.

Canon A-2, Agfa Ultra 50, f/11

FOREWORD

PilotPress Publishers and Twin Lights Publishers are pleased to bring you this photographic portrait.

The book presents many quality photographs of the White Mountains that is the work of amateur, semi-professional and professional photographers who submitted their work as part of a photographic contest.

These photographs are representative of the area. We ask that you view them with the same enthusiasm and excitement experienced by the photographers who live in or who visited the area and were prompted to record their memories on film.

We would like to congratulate all whose work was selected for this book and, in particular, we would like to highlight the following photographers:

FIRST PRIZE

Fall color on Mount Chocorua
Michael Hubley, Danvers, MA

Slanting rays of sunlight cast yet another perspective of fall's transforming beauty on Mt. Chocorua.
Nikon F5, 35-105mm, Fuji Velvia, f/22 Polarizer

Michael Hubley is an award-winning photographer whose passion for the great outdoors shows in his images. Although he loves the "Grand Vista" Michael believes one should learn to seek the beauty within. Largely self-taught through trial and error, he believes you never stop learning. Michael began his photography career in 1985 and stresses that it's never to late to learn.

Great Gulf Wilderness
Robert Kozlow, Lincoln, NH

The rugged beauty of the landscape and the personal achievement of "getting to the top" can be seen in this photo overlooking the Great Gulf Wilderness on Mt. Washington.
Minolta X-370, Fujichrome 100

Robert Kozlow, D.D.S. is a general dentist who has pursued scenic nature photography as a serious hobby for the last ten years. A 1984 graduate of the University of Michigan, School of Dentistry, Bob was given his first SLR camera as a graduation gift by his parents and has been exploring every region of New Hampshire ever since. Bob considers himself fortunate to live, work and hike in the White Mountains, where the quiet peace and awesome beauty of each season provides the perfect backdrop for unique photographic exploration through God's Country.

Sleigh Ride at Nestlenook Inn
Martin Harwood, Laconia, NH

A sleigh ride in Jackson gives passengers a chance to experience
what real horsepower feels like.
Minolta X-700, Velvia Film

Martin Harwood was born and grew up in Lebanon, New
Hampshire. He attended Norwich University and earned a
Bachelor's degree in economics and furthered his education
at Boston University earning a Master's degree. He served
in the army during both World War II and the Korean War.
Mr. Harwood is married with two daughters. In his professional career from which he is now retired, he taught in
New Hampshire public schools and served as Principal for
fifteen years. In addition to his avid interest in photography
that takes him throughout northern New England, he is a fly
fisherman and teaches fly tying in Laconia's adult
education program.

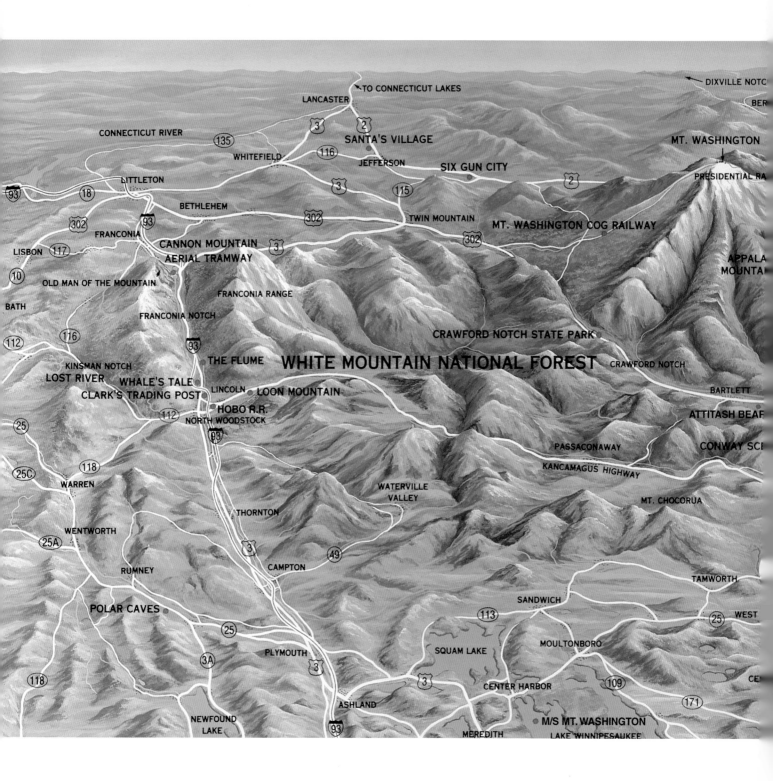

DIXVILLE NOTC

BER

TO CONNECTICUT LAKES

LANCASTER

MT. WASHINGTON

CONNECTICUT RIVER

135

SANTA'S VILLAGE

PRESIDENTIAL RA

WHITEFIELD

116

JEFFERSON

SIX GUN CITY

3

115

2

APPALA
MOUNTA

LITTLETON

93

18

BETHLEHEM

302

TWIN MOUNTAIN

MT. WASHINGTON COG RAILWAY

302

FRANCONIA

93

LISBON

117

CANNON MOUNTAIN
AERIAL TRAMWAY

3

302

10

BATH

OLD MAN OF THE MOUNTAIN

FRANCONIA RANGE

CRAWFORD NOTCH STATE PARK

112

116

FRANCONIA NOTCH

93

THE FLUME

WHITE MOUNTAIN NATIONAL FOREST

CRAWFORD NOTCH

CRAWFORD NOTCH

KINSMAN NOTCH

LOST RIVER

WHALE'S TALE

LINCOLN

LOON MOUNTAIN

BARTLETT

CLARK'S TRADING POST

112

HOBO R.R.

NORTH WOODSTOCK

ATTITASH BEAF

25

93

PASSACONAWAY

CONWAY SCI

25C

118

KANCAMAGUS HIGHWAY

WARREN

WATERVILLE
VALLEY

MT. CHOCORUA

WENTWORTH

THORNTON

25A

3

RUMNEY

49

TAMWORTH

CAMPTON

SANDWICH

POLAR CAVES

113

25

WEST

25

SQUAM LAKE

MOULTONBORO

3A

PLYMOUTH

3

3

109

CE

118

CENTER HARBOR

171

ASHLAND

NEWFOUND
LAKE

93

M/S MT. WASHINGTON

MEREDITH

LAKE WINNIPESAUKEE

The White Mountains - Birthplace of Legends

The White Mountains of New Hampshire are more than just 1,200 square miles, 86 peaks and nine notches, they are a place where classic New England scenes combine with one of natures most truly spectacular regions. It's an area that is part of where America began and is crowned by the fabled Presidential Range and the Northeast's highest peak, Mt. Washington. And that's only what meets the eye.

Amidst these small towns, mountains, valleys, lakes, waterfalls, rivers and covered bridges are the birthplaces of legends. There are so many stories, told and untold, all of which collectively give the White Mountains their unique character. These stories can be found around every bend, on each hilltop, along miles of stonewalls and in every village green.

Besides the ice ages and the rugged wilderness life of early Native Americans, we know discovery of this area began with the first White Mountain "tourist," Darby Field. In 1642, he and his Indian guides became the first men to climb Mt. Washington, a mountain considered to be the sacred dwelling place of the "Great Spirit." Darby didn't find his hoped-for gold and diamonds amidst the shining rock, just quartz, mica and timeless vistas.

For today's vacationers and explorers, the White Mountains continue to stand as silent sentinels, slowly marking the passage of time and perhaps most remarkably, offering the same awe-inspiring glimpses of beauty that have greeted generations past.

Throughout the ³/4 million-acre White Mt. National Forest and its environs are infinite images of breathtaking splendor. We share a marvelous cross-section of these images in this book, as seen through the eyes of photographers, amateur and otherwise, who have been inspired to capture the pictures you see in our collection.

While the pictures can't fully tell the story, you will be looking at scenes where the French-Indian War, the Revolutionary War and countless other historical moments took place in centuries past.

In more recent times, the White Mountains have become a region full of family attractions, ski areas and other modern amenities to complement the wilderness they surround and are a part of. This is a place where history has been made and is still in the making. A region that annually hosts more visitors than Yellowstone and Yosemite combined, but still offers the simplicity of finding a private spot in the woodlands all your own. It is the best of all worlds and is and will remain what the White Mountains have always stood for, the chance to choose your own trail.

Here is a true destination resort, and after nearly 200 years, the reasons why can still be seen, same as ever, just around the next bend.
-By Steven Caming

Publisher's Note: Steven Caming is the author of hundreds of newspaper and magazine feature stories about life and people in the White Mountains. He is also the producer of several historical documentaries that have appeared on PBS. He resides in Madison, New Hampshire.

Uta Teagan

An inspiring North Country sunset, as seen from Danforth Pond in Freedom.

Olympus Super Zoom 3000, Kodacolor print film, Kodak Gold

Southern
WHITE MOUNTAINS

Carolyn Bearce

Dow's Corner Antique Shop in
Tuftonboro appears ready to
do business in any century.
Wagon wheels, anyone?

Sears SLR 35mm, Kodak Gold 200, f/5.6

OPPOSITE

Ginny Messmore

The Sun's golden rays warm
the lakeside in Alton, as a
storm approaches in the distance.

Pentax K1000, Fuji Velvia

OPPOSITE

Linda Griffin

The Freedom Country Store, located in a historic turn-of-the-century building in where else? Freedom!

Minolta X-370, Fujichrome 100

ABOVE

Uta Teagan

Though it doesn't boast much of a Main St., the crossroads in Freedom Village are still a classic.

Olympus Super Zoom 3000,
Kodacolor print film, Kodak Gold

"Grant me the ability to be alone,
May it be my custom to go outdoors each day
Among the trees and grasses,
Among all the growing things
And there may I be alone,
And enter into prayer
To talk with the one
That I belong to."

RABBI NACHMAN OF BRATZLAV

Steven Caming

Back in the old shed after a
lifetime of service, this old
tractor has now become a
part of the Eaton landscape it
once shaped.

Patricia Osgood

Squam Lake (otherwise known
for its role in "On Golden
Pond") as seen from
Rattlesnake Mountain in
Holderness.

Pentax, Kodak 200

Steven Caming

A pastoral scene at the
Rockhouse Mountain Farm in
Eaton, at the onset of Autumn.

Michael Hubley

The Pemigewasset River offers hidden glimpses of fall beauty to those willing to get "off the beaten" path.

Nikon F5, 20mm, Fuji Velvia, f/22 Polarizer

OPPOSITE

Jennifer Hedda

This peaceful scene was captured on Russell Pond in the White Mountains National Forest just as foliage began to peak.

Autofocus camera, 35mm

BELOW

Frank Kaczmarek

Agassiz Basin in North Woodstock is one of many fine locations throughout the area to witness the effects of glacial runoff on local rivers.

Nikon FM2, 90mm, Fuji Velvia, f/22, 4sec

Robert Kozlow

Another remarkable vista of
the unspoiled Pemigewasset
Wilderness from Mt. Lincoln,
on the Franconia Ridge.

Minolta X-370, Fujichrome 100

*"The earth's distances invite the eye. And as
the eye reaches, so must the mind stretch to
meet these new horizons. I challenge anyone
to stand with Autumn on a hilltop and fail to
see a new expanse not only around him, but
in him, too."*

HAL BORLAND

ABOVE RIGHT

Robert Kozlow

The Pine Sentinal Covered Bridge in Lincoln is a hidden treasure waiting to be discovered!

Minolta X-370, Fujichrome 100

RIGHT

Martin Harwood

With Mt. Chocorua looming above, it casts a perfect reflection on a perfect fall day.

Minolta X-700, Velvia Film

Steven Caming

The Royal Lipizzan Stallions of
Austria make an annual visit to
Lincoln, where they astound
onlookers with dramatic "airs
above ground."

TOP

Michael Hubley

Autumn colors grace Lake
Chocorua, named for a leg-
endary Indian chief who leapt
from the distant mountain
peak that gives the lake its
name.

Nikon F5, 35-105mm, Fuji Velvia,
f/22 Polarizer

ABOVE

Robert Kozlow

This picture of Waterville
Valley is a perfect reflection of
what makes the White
Mountains-classic architecture,
water, mountains and time to
enjoy them!

Minolta X-370, Fujichrome 100

Patricia Osgood

The simplicity of January Bog in Campton in early winter is a timeless scene.

Pentax, Kodak 200

OPPOSITE ABOVE

Ginny Messmore

Ossippee Lake Marina, Ossippee, as summer wanes and the days grow shorter.

Pentax K1000, Fuji Velvia

OPPOSITE BELOW

Ginny Messmore

Dockside on New Hampshire's largest and perhaps most beautiful body of water, Lake Winnipesaukee.

Pentax K1000, Fuji Velvia

TOP

Raymond Turmelle

Chocorua Lake becomes a perfect reflecting pond from the shore along Route 16 at sunset.

Nikon FM, Kodak

ABOVE

Audrey Johns

Life in the White Mountains means having some unusual neighbors. This Black bear carefully empties the seeds without damaging the feeder, so he can return for more tomorrow!

Mark Georgian

A classic photo of New Hampshire's favorite summer visitor, the Loon. On Spectacle Pond.

Vivitar V2000, 300mm lens, f/5.6

Kristen Hand

"Forever Falls" offers a late autumn view of Rumney Falls as the cascading waters create a milky veil.

Olympus OM-PC. 180mm, Agfa XRG 400, f/22, 1/30

Kristen Hand

This vision of a bygone era was captured in Thornton, off Route 175. "Two Antiques" from a long gone past.

Olympus OM-PC. 40mm, Kodak gold 200, f/22. 1/125

ABOVE

Frank Kaczmarek

While this image is from North Woodstock, a keen eye could find this picture throughout the White Mountains. All it takes is birch, fungus and a few leaves!

Nikon FM2, 90mm, Fuji Velvia, f/22, 1/2sec

OPPOSITE

Raymond Turmelle

Another wonderful foliage view of Lake and Mt. Chocorua, in the afternoon sun.

Nikon FM, Kodak

BELOW

Steven Caming

Part of the 360° degree view on a hilltop in Eaton during the peak of foliage.

ABOVE LEFT

Robert Kozlow

The Bondcliff Trail in the
Pemigewasset Wilderness offers
scenic vistas in the world above
tree line.

Minolta X-370, Fujichrome 100

LEFT

Robert Kozlow

This view from Mt. Bondcliff
shows a good example of why
New Hampshire is referred to
as "The Granite State."

Minolta X-370, Fujichrome 100

Cal Carpenter

A winter morning sunrise, as seen from Moore's Pond in Tamworth. White-capped Mt. Chocorua can be seen in the distance.

Olympus Stylus, Kodak Gold 400

ABOVE

Martin Harwood

The North Country takes on a
crystal coating after a rare ice
storm, as seen here in Lincoln.

Minolta X-700, Velvia Film

LEFT

Robert Kozlow

A whimsical image of the
Flume Covered Bridge in
Lincoln, with Frosty the
Snowman guarding the way.

Minolta X-370, Fujichrome 100

OPPOSITE

Andrew Thompson

A quiet winter afternoon
with Wonalancet Chapel in
the foreground and Mt.
Whiteface behind.

Nikon N70, Nikon 75-300 zoom
@200mm, f/22 @ 1/15, Kodak Royal
Gold 100

Marilyn Thompson

The morning after a small snowstorm in Madison. Each tiny branch wears a white coat until the sun and wind strip it away.

Nikon One Touch 100, 35mm, 200ASA

Martin Harwood

A snowy "day after" at the historic Indian Head Cabins in North Woodstock. Nearby is the famous "Clark's Trading Post" and trained bear shows.

Minolta X-700, Velvia Film

David Burnham

The annual winter dogsled races on Lake Chocorua evoke a distant time when this was a good way to get around up here!

Anne McKnight de Rham

It seems a magical light is being cast over Lafayette and
Cannon mountains, in this view from Sugar Hill.

Olympus Multi F, Kodak 200

Western
WHITE MOUNTAINS

Michael Hubley

A Savannah Sparrow takes a breather atop a purple Lupine in Sugar Hill.

Nikon N90s, 75-300mm, Fuji Velvia, f/5.6

Vincent Parent

A patch of native Lupine, in all their glory, provides the perfect foreground for Mt. Lafayette in Sugar Hill.

Martin Harwood

This enticing country scene of a field of Lupines and a set of old wagon wheels can be found in Sugar Hill, if you know where and when to look!

Minolta X-700, Velvia Film

Len Wickens

The Flume in Franconia Notch is an exciting place-sheer granite walls, rushing waters and great footpaths to see it all!

Robert Kozlow

This stunning vista of Franconia Ridge in winter was taken from the heights of Cannon Mountain in the dawn's early light.

Minolta X-370, Fujichrome 100

"And this our life,
Exempt from public haunt,
Finds tongues in trees, books in the running brooks,
Sermons in the stones, and good in everything.
I would not change it."

WILLIAM SHAKESPEARE
(1564-1616)

ABOVE

Raymond Turmelle

The rushing waters of the Pemigewasset River carved the famous "Basin" in Franconia Notch. The massive cavity worn over countless centuries is now 40 feet in diameter and 28 feet deep!

Nikon FM, Kodak

OPPOSITE

Martin Harwood

Sugar Hill and Cannon Mountain combine with this image of classic New Hampshire as fall ends and winter approaches.

Minolta X-700, Velvia Film

Frank Kaczmarek

In the fog, Cascade Brook in Franconia Notch appears like a vision of an enchanted forest.

Nikon FM2, 24mm, Fuji Velvia, f/22,1sec

Frank Kaczmarek

This view of the "Basin" in Franconia Notch shows how water can work wonders, even on granite, given enough time.

Nikon FM2, 35-70mm, Fuji Velvia, f/22, 10sec

Frank Kaczmarek

This beautiful cascade of flowing waters can be found near Georgiana Falls, in the Franconia Notch area.

Nikon FM2, 35-70mm, Fuji Velvia, f/22, 2sec

Frank Kaczmarek

The simple serenity of this forest scene in Franconia Notch invites all who wish to partake.

Nikon FM2, 35-70mm, Fuji Velvia, f/16, 8sec

Angelo Costa

One of the better known, but less often seen residents of the North Country, Bullwinkle J. Moose is spotted here in Franconia.

OPPOSITE

Martin Harwood

This simple church in Sugar Hill says much about the type of New Englanders who still worship here. Simple, solid and classic.

Minolta X-700, Velvia Film

ABOVE

Martin Harwood

Opened in Bretton Woods in 1902, the Mt. Washington Hotel has a commanding view of the Presidential Range behind.

Minolta X-700, Velvia Film

RIGHT

Martin Harwood

As the seasons changed, the Mt. Washington Hotel in Bretton Woods opened for its first ever winter in the year 2000.

Minolta X-700, Velvia Film

Raymond Turmelle

An early winter view of Mt. Eisenhower from Gibbs Brook on Route 302 in the Bretton Woods area. Soon, all the land will wear a white blanket of snow.

Nikon FM, Kodak

Frank Kaczmarek

Besides its famous location, the Mt. Washington Hotel may be best known as the site of the WWII era Bretton Woods Monetary Conference.

Pentax 645, 120mm, Fuji Velvia, f/22, 1/15sec

ABOVE

Kristen Hand

Just around the bend from the
"Old Man of the Mountains"
in Franconia Notch. This
inviting scene seems to say:
"Your Canoe Awaits."

Olympus OM-PC. 40mm, Agfa HDC
200-2, f/22, 1/125

FOLLOWING PAGE

Robert Kozlow

A picture perfect fall day at
Lonesome Lake in Franconia
Notch with a dusting of snow
on the ridgeline behind.

Minolta X-370, Fujichrome 100

Robert Kozlow

Not much has changed at the Iris Farm in Sugar Hill over the years—and that's just the way they like it!

Minolta X-370, Fujichrome 100

Anne McKnight de Rham

Mountain farming in Sugar Hill shows a typical scene that plays itself out each growing season throughout family farms in the White Mountains.

Olympus Multi F, Kodak 200

Robert Kozlow

At the Sugar Hill Sampler, the North Country's bountiful harvest has been gathered together in this artistic display.

Minolta X-370, Fujichrome 100

OPPOSITE

Angelo Costa

In wintertime, the Franconia Notch State Park bicycle path provides an idyllic setting for a delightful afternoon of cross-country skiing.

RIGHT

Jan Zimmer

From high atop Cannon Mountain, this birds eye view takes in the tramway and panoramic mountains beyond.

Olympus 35mm, ED 35-135, IS-2DLX, Fuji Color asa200

BELOW

Michael Hubley

New Hampshire's favorite son, Daniel Webster, wrote this about the *Old Man of the Mountains* "Men hang out their signs indicative of their respective trades. Shoemakers hang out a gigantic shoe; jewelers, a monster watch; even the dentist hangs out a gold tooth; but up in the Franconia Mountains God Almighty has hung out a sign to show that in New England, He makes men."

Nikon N90s, 75-300mm, Fuji Velvia, f/8

COURTESY OF STEVEN CAMING COLLECTION

ABOVE

Robert Kozlow

St. Matthews Church in Sugar
Hill on a winters' day, stands
like a beacon of faith against
the coming storm.

Minolta X-370, Fujichrome 100

OPPOSITE

Robert Kozlow

A marvelous winter morning's
view of the Franconia Ridge as
seen from the summit of
Cannon Mountain.

Minolta X-370, Fujichrome 100

I think that I shall never see
A poem as lovely as a tree,
Poems are made by fools like me
But only God can make a tree.

JOYCE KILMER

OPPOSITE

Coren Milbury

The chilly granite ridgeline of Cannon Mountain as seen from Franconia Notch along I-93.

Kodak Gold 200-6, f/16

ABOVE

Robert Kozlow

Snow-capped Cannon Mountain provides this stunning view of Franconia Notch and Ridge

Minolta X-370, Fujichrome 100

ABOVE

Robert Kozlow

A hearty ice climber carefully makes his way up frozen Avalanche Falls in Franconia Notch. Man vs. Nature, both at their best.

Minolta X-370, Fujichrome 100

OPPOSITE

Robert Kozlow

In an annual rite of early spring, buckets gather sap a drop at a time to make the worlds' greatest maple syrup. This scene is in Bethlehem.

Minolta X-370, Fujichrome 100

Martin Harwood

This explosion of color and its mirror image were captured in Jefferson.

Minolta X-700, Velvia Film

Northern
WHITE MOUNTAINS

ABOVE

Martin Harwood

With nice, thick coats, these three friends are wintering over well in Jefferson, waiting for spring.

Minolta X-700, Velvia Film

OPPOSITE

G. Sharon White

This rare cluster of yellow Lady Slippers was discovered on Mt. Prospect in Lancaster.

Nikon FM-2, f/6

*"We sleep, but the loom of life never stops
And the pattern which was weaving when the
Sun went down is weaving when it comes up
Tomorrow."*

HENRY WARD BEECHER
(1813-1887)
SPENT AUG-OCT 1877 IN
THE WHITE MOUNTAINS.

Martin Harwood

Located in Jefferson, this heavenly church exemplifies the simple yet inspiring architecture of New England.

Minolta X-700, Velvia Film

Raymond Turmelle

The upper falls of the Ammonoosuc Brook, near the Cog Railway base road exemplifies the kind of hidden beauty that is everywhere in the White Mountains.

Nikon FM, Kodak

ABOVE

Martin Harwood

With the Presidential Range
off in the distance, these
llamas strike a handsome
pose in Jefferson.

Minolta X-700, Velvia Film

OPPOSITE

Robert Kozlow

The grandest of all remaining
Grand Hotels. The Balsams.
Viewed here from Table Rock
in Dixville Notch. The Balsams
boasts its own championship
golf course and ski area on its
15,000 acres.

Minolta X-370, Fujichrome 100

The Balsams, Dixville Notch, N. H.

ABOVE

Robert Kozlow

Way up in the Great North Woods, this country scene is in the village of West Stewartstown.

Minolta X-370, Fujichrome 100

OPPOSITE

Robert Kozlow

A panoramic view from atop Table Rock in Dixville Notch, just south of Colebrook.

Minolta X-370, Fujichrome 100

PREVIOUS PAGE

Robert Kozlow

A unique view of the church and bridge in Stark, a small but incredibly quaint little village.

Minolta X-370, Fujichrome 100

ABOVE

Raymond Turmelle

The picturesque Stark Covered Bridge spans the upper Ammonoosuc River. Stark is also home to the famous annual fiddler's contest.

Nikon FM, Kodak

OPPOSITE

Robert Kozlow

The setting sun casts long shadows over these hay rolls in Jefferson Meadows marking the end of another growing season.

Minolta X-370, Fujichrome 100

"—This curious world which we inhabit is more wonderful than it is convenient; more beautiful than it is useful; it is more to be admired and enjoyed than used."

HENRY DAVID THOREAU

David Evans
The shore of Conway Lake provides an
inviting view of an afternoon on the water.
Nikon 6006, Fuji Provia

Eastern
WHITE MOUNTAINS

ABOVE

Raphael Bustin

An engineering marvel as the world's first mountain climbing locomotive, the Cog Railway has been in continuous operation since it opened in 1869, taking adventurers to the top of Mt. Washington.

Nikon FE, Kodacolor

OPPOSITE

Martin Harwood

The Cog Railway begins its ascent of Mt. Washington along what was once a bridal path cut by the Crawford family in the early 1800's.

Minolta X-700, Velvia Film

COURTESY OF STEVEN CAMING COLLECTION

Mount Washington and Railroad

ABOVE

Michael Hubley

The Ellis River is one of many fed by runoff from Mt. Washington, creating pools and waterfalls all along its path.

Nikon F5, 24mm, Fuji Velvia, f/22

OPPOSITE

Robert Kozlow

The Great Gulf Wilderness on Mt. Washington is a 5,500-acre glacial cirque that has been forever protected from man's doings.

Minolta X-370, Fujichrome 100

FOLLOWING PAGE

David Evans

Mt. Washington, as seen from Conway Lake, on a perfectly still day. Even the snow-capped ridgeline, more than 50 miles away, reflects in the mirror-like surface.

Nikon 6006, Fuji Provia

"Over all the hilltops silence,
Among the treetops you feel hardly a breath
moving. The birds fall silent in the woods.
Simply Wait! Soon you too will be silent."

JOHANN WOLFGANG
VON GOATHE
(1749-1832)

Nora Bonosky

Whitton Pond in Albany on a summer day that seems to call you out to the dock. It's just a short swim.

Olympus C2002 Digital Camera f/10

Michael Hubley

Virtually any pull off along the Kancamagus Highway during foliage time will reward you with a view like this of the Swift River.

Nikon F5, 24mm, Fuji Velvia, f/22 Polarizer

David Evans

The Saco River is a favorite for exploring by canoe, as it offers water for all abilities and a great view around every bend.

Nikon 6006, Fuji Provia

Sandra Kunz

A simple yet compelling image of nature in progress. An older tree rots away as younger growth springs anew.

Canon Elan II, Fujicolor 200, f/8

Gregory Keeler

The Attitash Bear Peak Equine Festival brings world-class show jumping to the Mt. Washington Valley each summer.

Nikon N90, Ektachrome 100

Roxanne Kenerson

North Conway's Victorian gingerbread train station, in all its summer glory with yellow day lilies.

Canon EOS11, Velvia Slide film

Roxanne Kenerson

Zeb's General Store in North Conway not only looks the part, but also sells only New England goods.

Canon EOS11, Velvia Slide film

Len Wickens

The historic North Conway train station with its classic Victorian architecture is now the base of operations for the Conway Scenic Railroad.

Ricoh ASA 100

The Crawford Notch & Mt. Webster White Mountains, N. H.

Martin Harwood

Cascade Stream in Crawford Notch looking its very best on a blue sky, crisp fall day.

Minolta X-700, Velvia Film

ABOVE

Michael Hubley

While it meanders peacefully most of the year, the Swift River can become a raging torrent during Spring runoff. In Autumn, it's just plain beautiful.

Nikon F5, 75-300mm, Fuji Velvia, f/11

RIGHT

Len Wickens

The Crawford Notch Railroad station, first opened in the 1870's, still serves the public today as a stop for the Conway Scenic Railroad.

Robert Kozlow

Stone cairns like this help hikers find their way in the sometimes thick fog on Mt. Washington. This one is on the Crawford Path, which is part of the Appalachian Trail in one section.

Minolta X-370, Fujichrome 100

David Evans

Whether technical or freestyle, rock climbing is a popular pursuit in the White Mountains, as seen here on Square Ledge.

Nikon 6006, Fuji Provia

"Those who contemplate the beauty of the earth find reserves of strength that will endure as long as life lasts."

RACHEL CARSON
(1907-1964)

Sandra Kunz

An inviting trail on Mt. Crawford, up and into the mystical morning fog.

Canon Elan II, Fujicolor 200, f/16

Robert Kozlow

Enjoying a Fall afternoon out-doors at the Christmas Farm Inn in Jackson.

Minolta X-370, Fujichrome 100

Martin Harwood

Each year around harvest time, roadside produce stands, like this one in Conway, start popping up all over the White Mountains to share nature's bounty.

Minolta X-700, Velvia Film

"We shall never cease from exploration,
And the end of all our exploring,
Will be to arrive where we started,
And know the place for the first time."

T.S. ELIOT
(1888-1965)

The Haystacks above Bartlett, White Mountains, N. H.

Michael Hubley

This North Country beaver pond is typical of those found throughout the area, but at dawn they take on a special beauty.

Nikon N90s, 24mm, Fuji Velvia, f/22

Raymond Turmelle

Champney Falls, located off
the Kancamagus Highway was
named for Benjamin
Champney, founder of the
turn-of-the-century White
Mountain School of Art.

Nikon FM, Kodak

Robert Dennis

Just off the Kancamagus
Highway, coming from
Conway, the Rocky Gorge
scenic area can be found—
and it's worth the drive.

Nancy Page

One of the many easily
accessed beaches and swim-
ming holes along the shores of
the Saco. This one's in Conway.

ABOVE

David Evans

A full moon rises over Mt. Cranmore, with various slopes lit up for night skiing, in North Conway.

Nikon 6006, Fuji Provia

OPPOSITE

Robert Kozlow

If you want to ski Mt. Washington's Tuckerman Ravine, you have to earn it by walking up first. It's skiing the old fashioned way!

Minolta X-370, Fujichrome 100

ABOVE

F. Michael Bannon

Mt. Washington's Observatory Tower, coated in rime ice, has been the site of countless scientific experiments since the Observatory began round the clock measurements in 1932.

Pentax, Fujichrome

OPPOSITE

Colin Lowry

As the sun sets on another White Mountain winter, the maple sap buckets are hung in preparation for the sweetness of Spring.

Canon EOS Rebel G, Kodak 400, f/4.5

F. Michael Bannon

Mt. Washington's frozen
summit is the home of the
Observatory where the world's
highest winds were ever record-
ed: 231 mph in April 1934.

Pentax, Fujichrome

Robert Kozlow

A lone ice climber pits himself
against the challenge of ascend-
ing the frozen heights of
Crawford Notch.

Minolta X-370, Fujichrome 100

8695. SUMMIT HOUSE, MT. WASHINGTON. WHITE MOUNTAINS, N.H.

F. Michael Bannon

A classic shot of the original Summit Stage Office (which was the Observatory in 1934) covered in rime ice. Note the ice-covered chains used to hold the building down in high winds.

Pentax, Fujichrome

F. Michael Bannon

At 6,288 feet, Mt. Washington is the Northeast's highest peak, and can experience snow or rime ice (frozen vapor that grows into the wind, any month of the year).

Pentax, Fujichrome

David Evans

Known for the diverse ski areas in the region, skiers can find terrain to suit any ability, including the need for speed.

Nikon 6006, Fuji Provia

ABOVE

David Evans

Some folks are always looking
for a new way to enjoy the
slopes as seen on this snow
scoot at Mt. Cranmore.

Nikon 6006, Fuji Provia

ABOVE LEFT

Gregory Keeler

Big air and blue sky are the theme for this skier's dream at Attitash Bear Peak in Bartlett.

Nikon N90, Ektachrome 100

LEFT

David Evans

Story Land sometimes takes Cinderella's Pumpkin Coach out for a drive, as it did on this day at Mt. Cranmore.

Nikon 6006, Fuji Provia

ABOVE

David Evans

This snowboarder in North Conway seems to capture the spirit of freedom and adventure of the sport—a new kind of "flight without wings."

Nikon 6006, Fuji Provia

ACKNOWLEDGEMENTS

The publishers would like to acknowledge a few of the many people who helped with this book.

To the Mount Washington Valley Chamber of Commerce for their valuable advice. Visit their website at www.MountWashingtonValley.com.

Thanks to Steven Caming for the captions and additional images. Mr. Caming is a student of life in the White Mountains and his detailed knowledge of the area as well as his enthusiasm significantly expanded upon the images that we present here. Besides having written the introduction and captions for this book, Steven Caming is an award winning writer and an Independent Producer of several historical documentaries. He is currently working on an ongoing television series about the White Mountains called "North Country Journal."

Thanks to the Dick Hamilton and the White Mountains Attractions Association for the use of their map. Visit their welcome center in North Woodstock, New Hampshire, call them at (603) 745-8720 or visit their website at www.VisitWhiteMountains.com

And to Brenda Swithenbank for continued suggestions, support and encouragement.

F. Michael Bannon
Bartlett, NH 03812
(603) 374-6637
macbaney@moose.ncia.net
pp. 117, 118, 120, 121

Carolyn Bearce
Scituate, MA
p.14

Nora Bonosky
Brooklyn, NY
norabo@att.net
p. 92

David Burnham
Fairport, NY
djburnham@earthlink.com
p. 41

Raphael Bustin
288 Magnolia Avenue
Gloucester, MA 01930
rafeb@channel1.com
www.channel1.com/users/rafeb
p. 87

Steve Caming
RFD1, Box 167
Conway, NH 03818
(603) 447-6166
sagamore@landmarknet.net
pp. 20, 21, 26, 34, 49, 63, 76,
79, 87, 101, 108, 114, 118

Cal Carpenter
Bedford, MA
calcarp@tiac.net
p. 37

Angelo R. Costa
Franconia, NH 03580
pp. 53, 62

Robert A. Dennis
18 Orchard Crossing
Andover, MA 01810
(978) 470-1664
rad1212@aol.com
www.portimages.com
p. 112

David Evans
PO Box 1725
N. Conway, NH 03860
(603) 356-6025
images@davidevansphoto.com
www.davidevansphoto.com
pp. 84, 90, 94, 103, 114, 121, 125,
126(2)

Mark Georgian
57 Pearl Street
Amesbury, MA 01913
Urchin007@hotmail.com
p. 31

Linda L. Griffin
Naples FL 34112
(941) 732-3721
p. 16

Robert B. Hamilton
PO Box 291
Conway, NH 03818
603 447-3768
p. 4

Kristin Hand
Photos by Hand
65 Brockton Ave
Scituate, MA 02066
(781) 545-1635
pp. 32, 33, 57

Martin Harwood
186 Franklin Street
Laconia, NH 03246
pp. 9, 25, 38, 41, 46, 51, 54, 55(2),
70, 72, 75, 76, 86, 100, 106, 124

Jennifer Hedda
Medford, MA
jhedda@fas.harvard.edu
p. 23

Michael Hubley
7 River Drive
Danvers, MA 01923
(978) 774-1107
cover, pp. 7, 22, 27, 44, 63,
88, 93, 101, 109

Audrey Johns
East Hebron, NH
audrey@cyberportal.net
p. 30

Frank Kaczmarek
11 Vermont Drive
Oakdale, CT 06370
(860) 859-3578
Frank_S_Kaczmarek@groton.pfizer.com
pp. 22, 34, 52(3), 53, 56

Gregory Keeler
N Conway, NH
pp. 96, 126

Roxanne Kenerson
9 Lovewells Pond Road
Fryeburg, ME 04037
pp. 96, 97

Robert Kozlow
Lincoln, NH
pp. 8, 18, 24, 25, 27, 36(2), 38,
49, 58, 60, 61, 64, 65, 67, 68,
69, 77, 78, 79, 80, 83, 89, 102,
105, 115, 119, 122

Sandra Kunz
43 Oceanwoods Drive
Wickford, RI 02852
(401) 294-2305
Sandra_Kunz@brown.edu
pp. 95, 104

Colin J. Lowry
RR1, Box 84
Fryeburg, ME 04037
(207) 697-2002
ColinJLowry@hotmail.com
p. 116

Anne McKnight-deRham
Franconia, NH 03580
MdeRham@ncia.net
pp. 42, 60

Ginny Messmore
PO Box 1238
Dedham, MA 02027
(781) 255-8903
pp. 15, 29(2)

Coren A. Milbury
936 Bowman Drive
Lewes, DE 19958
302-644-0279
cmilbury@udel.edu
p. 66

David Nash
PO Box 290
Plymouth, NH 03264
(603) 536-4676
Jurassic@lr.net
p. 19

Patricia Osgood
Box 419
Campton, NH 03223
pp. 21, 28

Nancy Page
3 Putnam St
Sanford, ME 04073
(207) 324-2166
nancy@elmers.net
p. 110

Vincent J. Parent
20 Woodland Drive, #360
Lowell, MA 01852
(978) 452-2537
v.parent@neccsd.com
p. 45

Uta Teagan
Acton, MA 01722
pp. 12, 17, 82

Andrew Thompson
Wild Light Images
HC64, Box 257
Wonalancet, NH 03897
(603) 323-8304
p. 39

Marilyn Thompson
PO Box 975
N. Conway, NH 03860
p. 40

Ray Turmelle
14 Green Hill Road
Barrington, NH 03825
(603) 332-1857
pp. 30, 35, 50, 56, 74, 111

Len Wickens
The Joy of Photography
PO Box 5422
Magnolia, MA 01930
pp. 48, 98, 101

G. Sharon White
RR1, Box 543, Percy Road
N. Stratford, NH 03590
(603) 636-2188
p. 73

Jan Zimmer
PO Box 541
Lebanon, NH 03766
p. 63